ISBN 0 86112 546 0

© Brimax Books Ltd 1989. All rights reserved.
First published by BRIMAX, Newmarket, England 1989
Second printing 1990
Produced by Mandarin Offset
Printed in Hong Kong
The rhymes in this book have been
published as four separate titles:
Jack and Jill and other rhymes; Little Bo Peep
and other rhymes; Humpty Dumpty and other
rhymes; Old King Cole and other rhymes.
Rhymes selected and edited by Anne Finnis.
Designed by Brigitte Willgoss

Read a Rhyme

NURSERY RHYMES TO READ BY MYSELF

Illustrated by Pamela Storey

Brimax Books · Newmarket · England

Jack and Jill

Jack and Jill went up the hill
To fetch a pail of water;
Jack fell down and broke his crown,
And Jill came tumbling after.

Up Jack got, and home did trot,
As fast as he could caper,
He went to bed, to mend his head
With vinegar and brown paper.

Hey diddle diddle

Hey diddle diddle,
The cat and the fiddle,
The cow jumped over the moon;
The little dog laughed
To see such sport,
And the dish ran away with the spoon.

Little Jack Horner

Little Jack Horner
Sat in the corner,
Eating a Christmas pie;
He put in his thumb,
And pulled out a plum,
And said, "What a good boy am I!"

Hickory, dickory, dock

Hickory, dickory, dock,
The mouse ran up the clock.
The clock struck one,
The mouse ran down,
Hickory, dickory, dock.

Sing a song of sixpence

Sing a song of sixpence,
A pocket full of rye;
Four and twenty blackbirds,
Baked in a pie.

When the pie was opened,
The birds began to sing;
Was not that a dainty dish,
To set before the king?

The king was in his counting house,
Counting out his money;
The queen was in the parlour,
Eating bread and honey.

The maid was in the garden,
Hanging out the clothes,
There came a little blackbird,
And snapped off her nose.

Yankee Doodle

Yankee Doodle came to town,
Riding on a pony;
He stuck a feather in his cap
And called it macaroni.

Wee Willie Winkie

Wee Willie Winkie
  runs through the town,
Upstairs and downstairs
  in his night-gown,
Rapping at the window,
  crying through the lock,
Are the children all in bed,
  for now it's eight o'clock?

One, two, buckle my shoe

One, two,
Buckle my shoe;
Three, four,
Knock at the door;
Five, six,
Pick up sticks;
Seven, eight,
Lay them straight;
Nine, ten,
A big fat hen;

Eleven, twelve,
Dig and delve;
Thirteen, fourteen,
Maids a-courting;
Fifteen, sixteen,
Maids in the kitchen;
Seventeen, eighteen,
Maids in waiting;
Nineteen, twenty,
My plate's empty.

Jingle, bells!

Jingle, bells! Jingle, bells!
Jingle all the way;
Oh, what fun it is to ride
In a one-horse open sleigh.

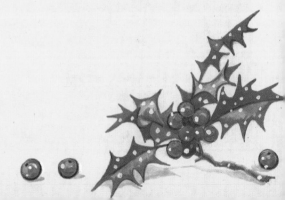

Old Mother Hubbard

Old Mother Hubbard
Went to the cupboard,
To fetch her poor dog a bone;
But when she came there
The cupboard was bare
And so the poor dog had none.

Bye, baby bunting

Bye, baby bunting,
Daddy's gone a-hunting,
Gone to get a rabbit skin
To wrap the baby bunting in.

Little Bo Peep

Little Bo Peep has lost her sheep,
And can't tell where to find them;
Leave them alone, and they'll come home,
And bring their tails behind them.

There was a crooked man

There was a crooked man,
  and he walked a crooked mile,
He found a crooked sixpence
  against a crooked stile;
He found a crooked cat,
  which caught a crooked mouse,
And they all lived together
  in a little crooked house.

There was a little girl

There was a little girl,
   and she had a little curl
Right in the middle
   of her forehead;
When she was good,
   she was very, very good,
But when she was bad,
   she was horrid.

Ring-a-ring o' roses

Ring-a-ring o'roses,
A pocket full of posies,
A-tishoo! A-tishoo!
We all fall down.

How many days

How many days has my baby to play?
Saturday, Sunday, Monday,
Tuesday, Wednesday, Thursday, Friday,
Saturday, Sunday, Monday.
Hop away, skip away,
My baby wants to play,
My baby wants to play every day.

The Queen of Hearts

The Queen of Hearts
She made some tarts,
All on a summer's day;
The Knave of Hearts
He stole the tarts,
And took them clean away.

The King of Hearts
Called for the tarts,
And beat the knave full sore;
The Knave of Hearts
Brought back the tarts,
And vowed he'd steal no more.

Lavender's blue

Lavender's blue, diddle, diddle,
Lavender's green;
When I am king, diddle, diddle,
You shall be queen.

Baa, baa, black sheep

Baa, baa, black sheep,
Have you any wool?
Yes, sir, yes, sir,
Three bags full;
One for the master,
And one for the dame,
And one for the little boy
Who lives down the lane.

Three little kittens

Three little kittens
   they lost their mittens,
And they began to cry,
Oh, mother dear, we sadly fear
That we have lost our mittens.
What! Lost your mittens,
   you naughty kittens!
Then you shall have no pie.
Mee-ow, mee-ow, mee-ow.
No, you shall have no pie.

The three little kittens
  they found their mittens,
And they began to cry,
Oh, mother dear, see here, see here,
For we have found our mittens.
Put on your mittens,
  you silly kittens,
And you shall have some pie.
Purr-r, purr-r, purr-r,
Oh, let us have some pie.

Three blind mice

Three blind mice, see how they run!
They all ran after the farmer's wife,
Who cut off their tails with a carving knife,
Did you ever see such a thing in your life,
As three blind mice?

Twinkle, twinkle, little star

Twinkle, twinkle, little star,
How I wonder what you are!
Up above the world so high,
Like a diamond in the sky.

Humpty Dumpty

Humpty Dumpty sat on a wall,
Humpty Dumpty had a great fall.
All the king's horses,
And all the king's men,
Couldn't put Humpty together again.

The animals went in two by two

The animals went in two by two,
Hurrah! Hurrah!
The animals went in two by two,
Hurrah! Hurrah!

The animals went in two by two,
The elephant and the kangaroo,
And they all went into the ark,
For to get out of the rain.

Ding, dong, bell

Ding, dong, bell,
Pussy's in the well.
Who put her in?
Little Johnny Green.
Who pulled her out?
Little Tommy Stout.
What a naughty boy was that,
To try to drown poor pussy cat.

Little Miss Muffet

Little Miss Muffet
Sat on a tuffet,
Eating her curds and whey;
There came a big spider,
Who sat down beside her
And frightened Miss Muffet away.

I had a little pony

I had a little pony,
His name was Dapple Gray;
I lent him to a lady
To ride a mile away.

One, two, three, four, five

One, two, three, four, five,
Once I caught a fish alive,
Six, seven, eight, nine, ten,
Then I let it go again.

Why did you let it go?
Because it bit my finger so.
Which finger did it bite?
This little finger on the right.

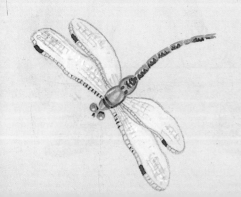

Rain, rain, go away

Rain, rain, go away,
Come again some other day;
Little Johnny wants to play.

Mary, Mary, quite contrary

Mary, Mary, quite contrary,
How does your garden grow?
With silver bells and cockle shells,
And pretty maids all in a row.

Oranges and lemons

Oranges and lemons,
Say the bells of St. Clement's.

You owe me five farthings,
Say the bells of St. Martin's.

When will you pay me?
Say the bells of Old Bailey.

When I grow rich,
Say the bells of Shoreditch.

When will that be?
Say the bells of Stepney.

I'm sure I don't know,
Says the great bell at Bow.

Here comes a candle
    to light you to bed,
Here comes a chopper
    to chop off your head.

I had a little nut tree

I had a little nut tree,
Nothing would it bear
But a silver nutmeg
And a golden pear;

The King of Spain's daughter
Came to visit me,
And all for the sake
Of my little nut tree.

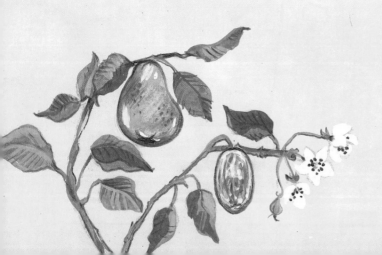

Little Betty Blue

Little Betty Blue
Lost her holiday shoe,
What can little Betty do?
Give her another
To match the other,
And then she may walk out in two.

Rock-a-bye, baby

Rock-a-bye, baby, on the tree top,
When the wind blows
　　the cradle will rock;
When the bough breaks
　　the cradle will fall,
Down will come baby, cradle, and all.

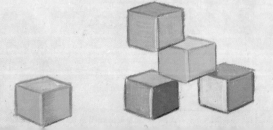

Old King Cole

Old King Cole
Was a merry old soul,
And a merry old soul was he;
He called for his pipe,
And he called for his bowl,
And he called for his fiddlers three.

Every fiddler, he had a fiddle,
And a very fine fiddle had he;
Twee tweedle dee, tweedle dee,
   went the fiddlers.
Oh, there's none so rare
As can compare
With King Cole and his fiddlers three.

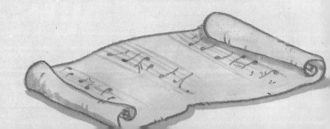

Little Boy Blue

Little Boy Blue,
Come blow your horn,
The sheep's in the meadow,
The cow's in the corn;
But where is the boy
Who looks after the sheep?
He's under a haystack,
Fast asleep.
Will you wake him?
No, not I,
For if I do,
He's sure to cry.

Pussy cat, pussy cat

Pussy cat, pussy cat,
   where have you been?
I've been to London
   to look at the queen.
Pussy cat, pussy cat,
   what did you there?
I frightened a little mouse
   under her chair.

Pat-a-cake, pat-a-cake

Pat-a-cake, pat-a-cake, baker's man,
Bake me a cake as fast as you can;
Pat it and prick it, and mark it with B,
Put it in the oven for baby and me.

There was an old woman

There was an old woman
  who lived in a shoe,
She had so many children
  she didn't know what to do;
She gave them some broth
  without any bread;
She whipped them all soundly
  and put them to bed.

Chook, chook, chook

Chook, chook, chook,
Good morning Mrs Hen
How many chickens have you?
Madam, I have ten.

Four of them are yellow,
Four of them are brown,
Two of them are speckled,
The nicest in the town.

This little pig

This little pig went to market,
This little pig stayed at home,
This little pig had roast beef,
This little pig had none,
And this little pig cried,
Wee-wee-wee-wee-wee,
All the way home.

Mary had a little lamb

Mary had a little lamb,
Its fleece was white as snow;
And everywhere that Mary went
The lamb was sure to go.

It followed her to school one day,
That was against the rule;
It made the children laugh and play
To see a lamb at school.

The north wind doth blow

The north wind doth blow,
And we shall have snow,
And what will poor robin do then?
Poor thing.
He'll sit in a barn,
And keep himself warm,
And hide his head under his wing.
Poor thing.

Cock a doodle doo

Cock a doodle doo!
My dame has lost her shoe,
My master's lost his fiddlestick,
And knows not what to do.

I see the moon

I see the moon,
And the moon sees me;
God bless the moon,
And God bless me.